Step into the world of . . .

Sea Raiders
and
Pirates

Contents

Ahoy There, Me Hearties!

What do you imagine when you think of pirates? Giant ships and treasure maps? Parrots, eye patches and swords? Perhaps all these things. But pirates were not just daring explorers seeking fame and fortune. Some were brutal, merciless sea-robbers, and were very dangerous to know!

Thieves at Sea

The word "pirate" means "a person who attacks and robs ships at sea", but there were actually many different types of pirate.

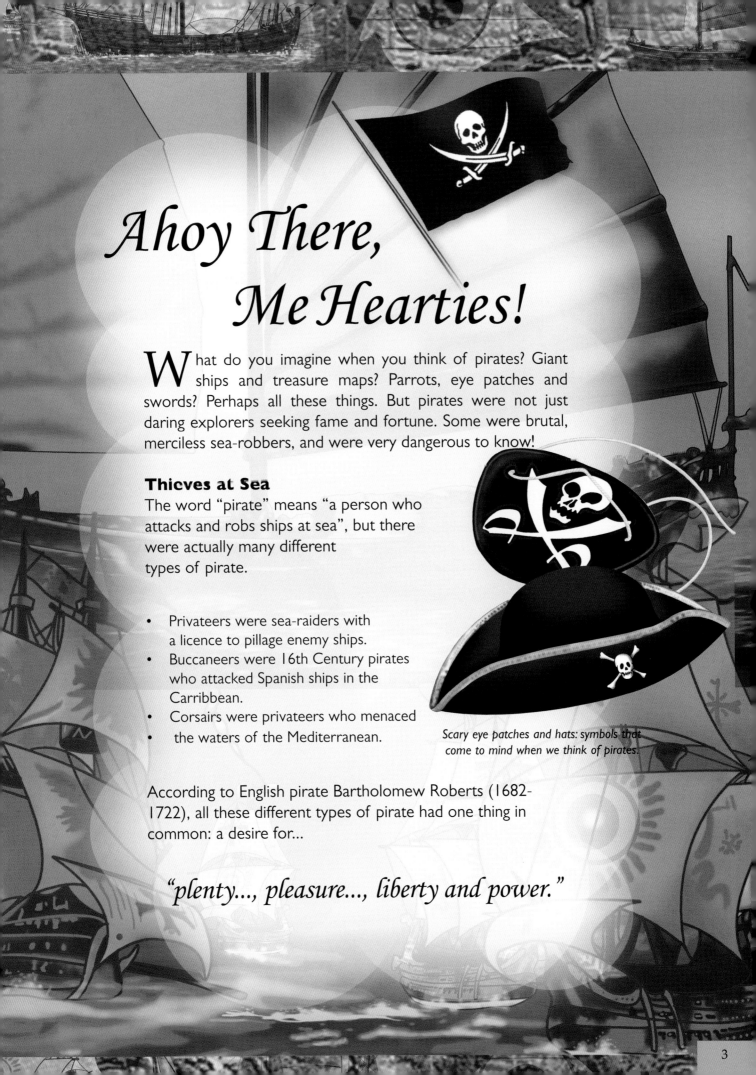

- Privateers were sea-raiders with a licence to pillage enemy ships.
- Buccaneers were 16th Century pirates who attacked Spanish ships in the Carribbean.
- Corsairs were privateers who menaced
- the waters of the Mediterranean.

Scary eye patches and hats: symbols that come to mind when we think of pirates.

According to English pirate Bartholomew Roberts (1682-1722), all these different types of pirate had one thing in common: a desire for...

"plenty..., pleasure..., liberty and power."

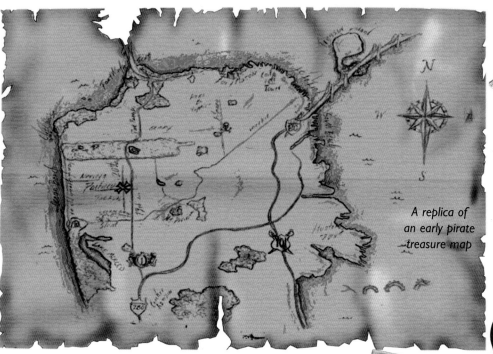

A replica of an early pirate treasure map

Who were Corsair

Corsairs were seamen privateers from France who sai mostly on the Mediterranean S Some corsairs, like the Barbar Corsairs of North Africa, wer supported by their governmer to attack enemy ships!

Did pirates really have treasure maps?

Treasure maps, with a big 'X' to mark the spot of buried treasure, are among the most fascinating part of pirate lore. Many believe that such maps never existed – except in story books and movies! William Kidd is one of the few pirates known to have buried treasure. In 1699 he buried a stash of gold, silver, jewels, sugar and silks on an island just off New York. Many believed that Kidd had buried more treasure elsewhere, but it has never been discovered!

What does the word 'pirate' mean?

'Pirate' means someone who raids at sea. It is thought that the word *'peirato'* was first used around 140 BC by Polybius, an historian, however, it is widely believed that the Greek historian Plutarch gave the first real definition of piracy. He wrote that pirates were those who attacked ships and maritime cities without legal authority.

Buccaneers became famous for their wild behaviour and acts of cruelty.

How were privateers different from pirates?

Like pirates, privateers also attacked other vessels and stole valuables from them. However, they were different from pirates because they were given a special licence from their government to raid and capture pirate ships. This licence was known as a 'Letter of Marque'. Many privateers decided to become pirates when they realised how much money their pirate enemies had!

What kind of clothes did pirates wear?

Pirates often dressed in bright clothes that did not necessarily match! Of course, most pirates usually wore old and tattered clothes, but they changed if they managed to steal better outfits. The leader sometimes wore clothes made from costly silks that he looted from merchant ships.

Were the Vikings also pirates?

The Vikings of Scandinavia were fierce warriors who travelled to different parts of the world over 1,000 years ago. Although they raided many ships for treasure, not all Vikings were pirates. Most were sailors in search of land to settle on.

Were there pirates in all parts of the world?

Pirates have been looting ships for years, in many different parts of the world. Pirates were active in the Mediterranean, Asia, Africa, Europe and the Americas.

One of the dressed pirates was ack Bart, who wore tcoats, breeches and huge red feather in his hat!

FACT BOX

- Nassau in the Bahamas was the heart and capital of the Golden Age of Piracy.

- Pirates could become rich overnight, plundering gold and costly goods from merchant vessels. They would carry their wealth around in little pouches, and wasted no time in spending it!

Pirates were not the greatest money-savers and spent most of what they looted very quickly indeed!

- Barbary corsairs were Islamic pirates who fought Christian corsairs in the Mediterranean Sea. They either got their name from their European enemies, who called them 'barbaric', or were named after their native Barbary Coast of North Africa.

What was the Jolly Roger?

The Jolly Roger flag is probably the most well known symbol of the pirate world. The flag, with a white skull and pair of crossbones on a black background, was used by many pirates throughout the 18th Century. The Jolly Roger was meant to arouse fear in the enemy!

Pirates often referred to the Jolly Roger as Captain Death!

Why did some people choose to become pirates?

People became pirates for many reasons. Some turned to piracy when their own ships were captured. Others joined pirate crews after serving as privateers. The lack of jobs after wars also forced many unemployed sailors to turn to piracy.

Why did piracy start to fade away in the late 1800s?

Pirate activity began to decline in the 19th Century for a variety of reasons. Firstly, better ocean surveillance by naval vessels made it more difficult for pirates to attack. The widespread acceptance of piracy as a major crime also helped to prevent raids; many captured pirates were publicly hanged to deter others from taking up a life of crime!

Did pirates really like to drink lots of alcohol?

Supplies of water on board a ship were limited, and quickly went bad so sailors drank bottled beer, rum, or grog. Grog was water mixed with rum - the rum disguised the taste of the stale water and helped to preserve it!

The association between pirates and rum is so strong that a common nickname for rum is 'the pirate's drink'!

Long, Long Ago...

Thousands of years ago, man began to sail to different lands for trade. As more and more people took to the oceans, tales of the pirate world began to unfold...

Proof of Pirates

The might of early sea raiders is evident in ancient myths and legends. One such myth tells us about Dionysus, the Greek God of Wine. Captured by pirates, Dionysus changed into a lion to scare his kidnappers, who jumped into the sea in fright. To punish them further, Dionysus turned the pirates into dolphins! This tale lives on through ancient documents, mosaics and ceramic paintings.

An ancient Greek wine cup painted with the myth of Dionysus.

And Off They Sailed...

As bigger and better ships were built, pirates from all around the world started a new regime of crime and terror. Pirates of the Mediterranean and Aegean Seas even established their own pirate empires! Vikings voyaged across the Atlantic and invaded many of the coastal cities of Europe, and Japanese and Chinese sea robbers terrorised the coasts and waters of Asia. Soon piracy became a threat for merchant ships everywhere! Pirates, with their savage ways, were certainly here to stay!

How old is the practice of piracy?

There is no clear date to mark the beginning of piracy, but it is known that pirates existed in ancient civilisations. One of the first documents to mention pirates dates back to 1350 BC. It was a report carved into a clay tablet describing shipping attacks in North Africa.

Why did people fear the Barbary corsairs?

The Barbary corsairs first set sail from the southern coast of the Mediterranean, which became known as the Barbary Coast, at the time of the Crusades. The Crusades were holy wars that broke out at the end of the 11th Century between Christians and Muslims.

Corsairs targeted Christian ships bound for the Crusades and would capture the wealthy knights on board. They would strip the crew of their clothes and belongings, and force them to work as slaves. The most famous Barbary corsairs acquired fearsome reputations throughout Europe and became heroes in the Islamic world.

Some countries negotiated treaties with the Corsair states to protect their citizens from the terrifying Barbabry pirates.

Who were the Phoenicians?

The Phoenicians were some of the earliest known pirates. Although they were legal traders in the Mediterranean, they occasionally looted merchant ships and towns along the coast.

Who was Polycrates?

Polycrates was a Greek dictator who forcefully took over the ancient city of Samos. He owned a fleet of 100 pirate ships!

Polly want a cracker?

The turtles of the Caribbean Sea were a common source of meat for pirates while sailing. They were easy to catch, because they moved slowly. They were said to taste quite good, too!

Why did ancient Greek pirates like the Aegean Sea?

Much of the ancient Greek civilisation developed around the Aegean Sea. Greek pirates used this to their advantage. They hid on the Aegean islands and took merchant ships by surprise!

Did ancient pirates use stone catapults to fire at enemy ships?

Ancient pirates used a variety of weapons for battles at sea and on land. It is believed that the Ancient Greek and Roman pirates used stone catapults to attack their enemies! In 2003, archaeologists discovered stone catapults at the ancient island-city of Antikythera in Greece.

FACT BOX

- King Shapur of Persia (309-379 AD) was known for waging battles against pirates in the Persian Gulf. Legend has it that he pierced the shoulders of the pirates he captured, and roped them all together! For this he earned the nickname, "Zulaklaf", which means "Lord of the Shoulders!"

- Ancient Greek and Roman pirates often painted eyes on their ships for good luck! They believed that the eyes of their gods and goddesses would protect them from dangers ahead.

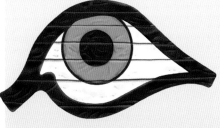

The painting of eyes on ancient sailing vessels may have originated in ancient Egypt.

Stone catapults were also known as ballistas and featured quite commonly on pirate ships.

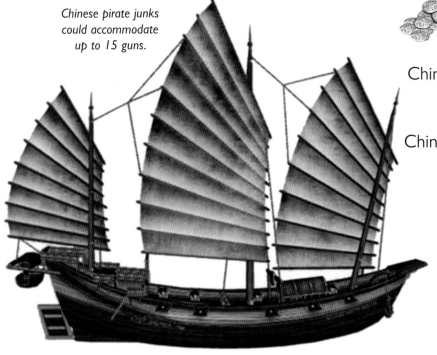

Chinese pirate junks could accommodate up to 15 guns.

What kind of sailing vessel did ancient Chinese pirates use?

Chinese pirates sailed in junks to allow for eas[y] and fast movement. Junks were also good for tricking enemy ships. Most Chinese merchants also sailed in junks, so it w[as] difficult for them to spot a pirate junk until it was much too late!

Were there any laws aga[inst] piracy in ancient times?

A law against piracy did exist in ancie[nt] Rome. It was recorded in a document [of] rules for dealing with pirates, dating ba[ck] to 100 BC.

How organised were pirates in ancient China?

The pirates of ancient China were known to be very well organised. They kept records and drew up contracts for everything, even keeping records of the payments they received from their victims!

Who were the corsairs of Malt[a]

The corsairs of Malta fought against th[e] Barbary corsairs. They helped the Knights of Malta to wage wars against Islamic invaders, but, gradually, they too were lured in by the riches of piracy!

What kind of ships did ancient Greek and Roman pirates use?

Greek and Roman pirates used galleys called **Triremes** to ram holes into enemy ships. Triremes were lightweight and had shallow bottoms, which made them fast and easy to move.

The trireme represented the sea power of the pirates of ancient Greece.

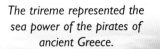

Women Pirates

The 18th Century worlds of business, art, and politics were dominated by men, and so too was piracy. But there were women who dreamed of sailing the Seven Seas, and who did so, having learned to dress, drink, swear, and fight like their fellow pirates!

Hidden in History

Historical accounts about women pirates differ. One writer suggests that Mary Read and Anne Bonny, like many others in their situation, hid their true identities from their fellow crew members right up until the moment of their trial (both escaped the death penalty because they were pregnant). Other eyewitnesses claim that women only disguised themselves in men's clothes for fighting. What is certain is that many female pirates have escaped the notice of history: we only know about the ones who, like Read and Bonny, eventually revealed themselves.

Here are the stories of just some of the brilliant women pirates who proved themselves to be just as fierce and fearless as their male counterparts...

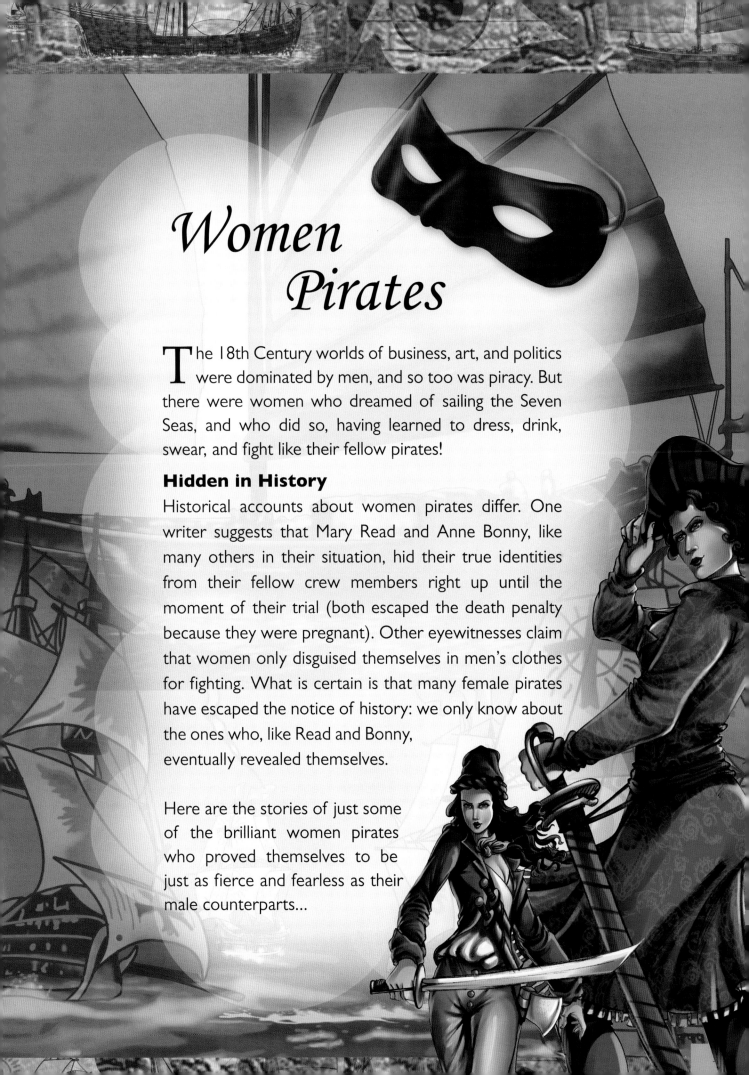

Mary Read
(also known as Mark Read)

Born: 1685, England

Died: 1721, Spanish Town, Jamaica

Mary Read fought in both the English army and the navy disguised in men's clothes. When her ship was captured by pirates, she decided to join them!

Read was known for her bravery: during one attack all but one of her fellow pirates hid, while she and Anne Bonny fought their enemies by themselves. When the cowards refused to come out and fight alongside them, Mary Read shot them!

Anne Bonny

Born: 1702, Republic of Ireland

Died: 1782, South Carolina, USA

When Anne Bonny met the pirate Jack Rackham, she left her sailor husband and embarked on a life of piracy, dressed as a man!

Like Mary Read, Anne Bonny was a fearsome fighter. When Rackham was eventually caught and sentenced to death, Bonny told him: *"Had you fought like a man, you need not have been hanged like a dog!"*

Alvilda

Born: Unknown

Died: Unknown

Alvilda was a Swedish Goth, and one of the first female pirate captains. She went to sea with an all-woman crew to escape an arranged marriage to the Danish Prince Alf!

FACT BOX

■ Pirates often relied upon stealing everyday necessities, like food and medicine, from the ships they raided. In 1720, one victim who survived his ordeal remembered that: *"No part of the cargo was so much valued by the robbers as the doctor's chest, for they were all poxed to a great degree."*

Tricorn hats were round-rimmed hats with three turned up corners.

■ Gambling for money was forbidden on board most pirate ships, because it often caused rows and fighting! Pirates were allowed to gamle their ill gotten gains when they reached dy land, and often lost fortunes at card games!

Which woman pirate led a group of more than 50,000 pirates?

Cheng I Sao of China was one of the most famous woman pirates. She took charge of more than 50,000 pirates in the early 19th Century!

Ching Shih

Born: 1775, Guangdong, China

Died: 1844, Guangzhou, China

The China Sea was terrorised in the early 19th Century by a huge pirate fleet commanded by Ching Shih, who controlled 1,800 ships and around 80,000 pirates!

Charlotte de Berry

Born: 1636, England

Died: Unknown

Dressed as a man, Charlotte de Berry followed her husband into the English Navy but was kidnapped and foreced aboard a vessel bound for Africa. Brave Charlotte led a mutiny and took over the ship, which she captained as it sailed the African coast, capturing gold ships!

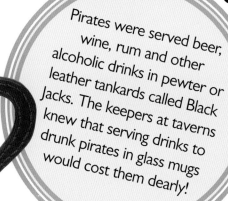

Polly want a cracker?

Pirates were served beer, wine, rum and other alcoholic drinks in pewter or leather tankards called Black Jacks. The keepers at taverns knew that serving drinks to drunk pirates in glass mugs would cost them dearly!

Bloodthirsty Buccaneers

Originally hunters from the Caribbean island of Hispaniola, buccaneers were a fierce band of bloodthirsty pirates who obeyed no laws except their own. They maintained order on board their ships with gruesome acts of cruelty, swelling their numbers by accepting convicts, outlaws and excaped slaves to their brutal band of brothers.

Buccaneer Island

For many years the buccaneers lived peacefully on the island of Hispaniola (modern day Haiti and Dominican Republic), hunting the animlas that lived there. When the Spanish attacked them, the buccaneers formed the "Brotherhood of the Coast" to defend themselves. Some moved to the tiny neighbouring island of Tortuga, which gave them an excellent vantage point from which to prey on Spanish ships.

The parrot became a major symbol of the pirate world thanks to Long John Silver, the fictional character from Treasure Island.

Bloodthirsty Buccaneers

How did the Buccaneers get their name?

Living peacefully on Hispaniola, the Arawak Indians taught the buccaneers how to cure their meat in smokehouses called "boucans". This is how the "boucaniers" got their name!

What famous weapon did the Buccaneers reportedly invent?

According to legend, the cutlass was invented by buccaneers. They used these long knives to butcher their meat for the boucan. Over time, they evolved into the short swords famously used by seamen.

According to pirate legend, the cutlass was invented by early Buccaneers, who used long, slightly curved knives to butcher their meat!

Did Buccaneers always have such fierce reputations?

Even when they lived peacefully as hunters, buccaneers had wild reputations. They used to wear uncured hides of pigs and cows they slaughtered, and were stinking and bloody from their work!

Famous Buccaneers

Bartholomew Portugues

Portugues managed to escape from a prison ship, despite not being able to swim! This ingenious buccaneer splashed to shore using wine jars for floats!

Sir Henry Morgan

Welshaman Morgan was the most famous of the buccaneers. He was just as cruel as the rest of his band, but his fearles attacks on Spanish colonies won him an English knighthood and the governorship of Jamaica!

Francis L'Ollonais

French Buccaneer Francis L'Ollonais was the meanest of a mean gang. He was so feared by the Spanish that they would prefer to die rather than surrender to this cruel pirate. He tortured his captives mercilessly before cutting them into pieces. It was even said that, on one occassion, he cut out the heart of a Spanish prisoner and stuffed it into the mouth of another!

Rock Braziliano

Braziliano was a drunkard, named after his lengthy exile in Brazil. He once spit roasted two Spanish farmers who refused to give him their pigs for food!

FACT BOX

- Every pirate ship was home to a population of rats. These furry stowaways could cause real problems for the crew: they helped themselves to their limited supply of food, and could even gnaw their way through the hull of the ship and sink it!

- Pirates often killed the rats on board their ships to try to keep their numbers down. One Spanish Galleon reported the killing of over 4,000 rats on a voyage from the Carribean to Europe!

- Describing the rather questionable table manners of a band of starving buccaneers, Alexander Exquemerling wrote: "Such was their hunger that they more resembled cannibals than Europeans...the blood many times running down from their beards."

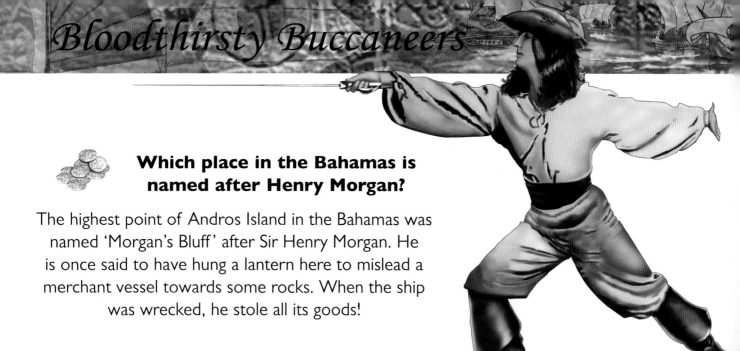

Bloodthirsty Buccaneers

Which place in the Bahamas is named after Henry Morgan?

The highest point of Andros Island in the Bahamas was named 'Morgan's Bluff' after Sir Henry Morgan. He is once said to have hung a lantern here to mislead a merchant vessel towards some rocks. When the ship was wrecked, he stole all its goods!

Which famous smuggling gang was named after their home village?

The Hawkhurst Gang (1735 - 1749) was a famous gang of smugglers named after the English village they called home!

Who is considered to be one of the most cruel pirates ever to have lived?

Edward Low, a Caribbean pirate, was famous for his cruel ways. It is believed that he cut off people's lips or ears when he wanted to punish them!

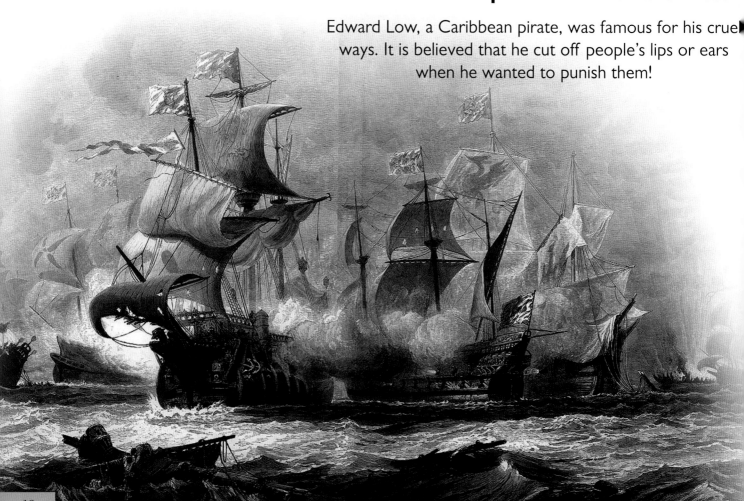

All Aboard!

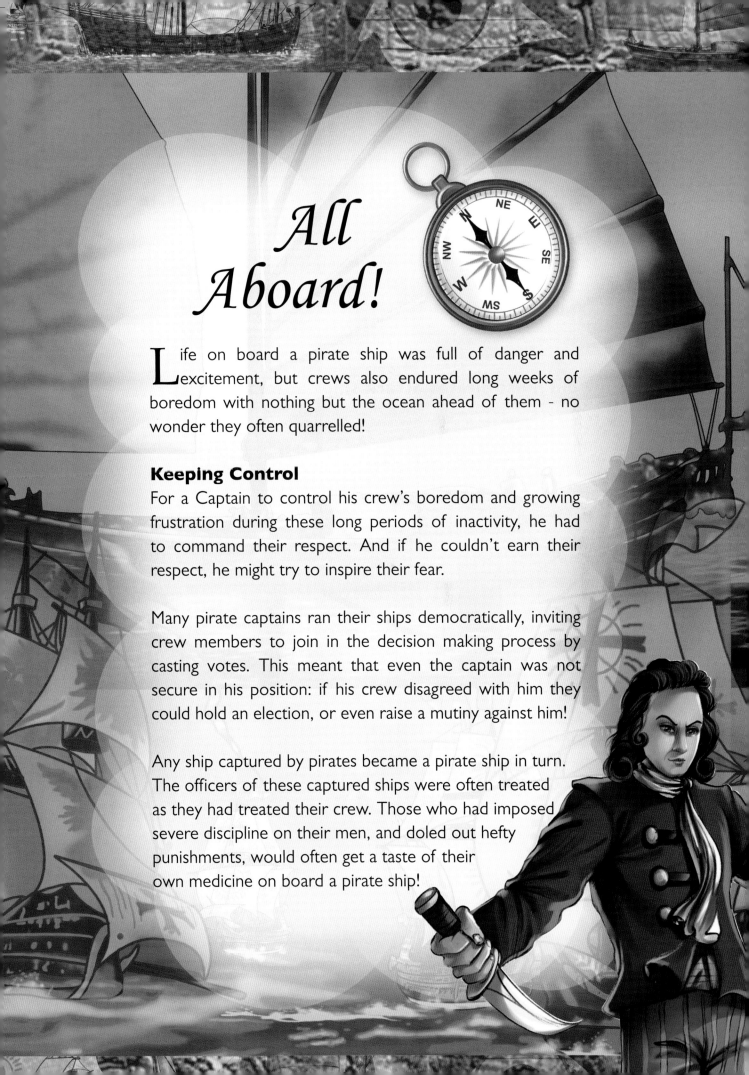

Life on board a pirate ship was full of danger and excitement, but crews also endured long weeks of boredom with nothing but the ocean ahead of them - no wonder they often quarrelled!

Keeping Control

For a Captain to control his crew's boredom and growing frustration during these long periods of inactivity, he had to command their respect. And if he couldn't earn their respect, he might try to inspire their fear.

Many pirate captains ran their ships democratically, inviting crew members to join in the decision making process by casting votes. This meant that even the captain was not secure in his position: if his crew disagreed with him they could hold an election, or even raise a mutiny against him!

Any ship captured by pirates became a pirate ship in turn. The officers of these captured ships were often treated as they had treated their crew. Those who had imposed severe discipline on their men, and doled out hefty punishments, would often get a taste of their own medicine on board a pirate ship!

How did pirates find their way at sea?

Navigation was fairly primitive throughout the Golden Age of Piracy, so pirates and seamen alike relied on a combination of geographical knowledge, common sense, and good luck!

The telescope, nicknamed the "bring 'em near", was invented in the late 16th Century and fast became a vital navigation tool. Even when pirates could not spy land, they could judge its direction and distance fairly accurately by observing clouds and sea birds.

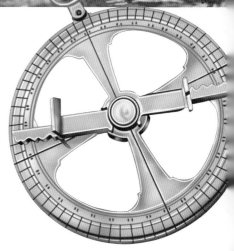

Without the astrolabe, pirates would have h[...] difficult time figuring out where their ship was[...]

How did most pirates attack ships at mid-sea?

Every pirate crew had their own way of attacking vessels, but most liked to take their enemy by surprise. They would board the ship quickly by jamming its rudder, so it could not move. Pirates also used their weapons to attack any victims who tried to put up a fight.

Pirates boarded the enemy ship with grappling hooks, axes, ropes and pulleys

Essentially trading ships, caravels could carry over 1,000 kg (100 tonnes) of cargo! This made them useful for pirates, who travelled in large numbers and with many heavy weapons.

- Sloops were the most common ships used by pirates to sail the waters of the Caribbean. They had large sails stretched across a single mast, which made them fast and easy to move. An average sloop could carry about 75 pirates!

What kind of ships did pirates sail in?

Pirates sailed in all kinds of vessels. Some of the most popular included brigantines, sloops, schooners, junks, galleys and caravels. Caravels were lightweight ships that were useful for pirates, as they could sail fast, even against strong winds. They could also carry a lot of goods.

Did pirates follow any rules at sea?

Most pirates followed a certain code of conduct while at sea. The rules included putting out all the lights by eight o'clock at night and keeping their weapons clean and ready for use at all times.

- Pirates commonly ate hardtack at sea. This was a dry and extremely hard biscuit, made from flour, water, and, sometimes, salt. Pirates soaked the biscuits in water or broke it into small pieces which they washed down with grog – a mixture of rum, warm water and lemon.

Hardtack did not spoil easily! This meant it was suitable for long sea journeys, but the biscuits sometimes became infested with weevils (beetles)!

What rights did pirate crew members have?

Each pirate was allowed to vote on which ships to attack or where to go. Crew members also had the right to elect a new leader, if they felt that the existing captain was not good enough!

What did pirates sign before they officially became crew members?

All pirates had to sign an agreement before they became members of a crew. The agreement contained articles, which included information about how much the pirate would be paid, what he was allowed and forbidden to do, and what punishments he could expect for breaking rules.

Was the captain of a pirate ship very powerful?

The captain of a pirate ship was the person who owned and sailed the ship. The head of the pirate crew was only the leader of his group during battles and not the commander of the ship. He was elected by his crew members and made the decisions reagrading boarding and attacking enemy ships or raiding lands. The captain, who steered the vessel, received the same amount of booty as the leader.

Did the pirate captain have his own cabin?

Most pirates slept in cramped quarters below deck. The captain had his own cabin in the quarterdeck, where the helm (steering wheel) of the ship was. The captain's cabin was usually small but well equipped, with a desk, maps, a globe, and navigational tools. Everyone was allowed to use the captain's cabin.

What happened to pirate captains if they failed to steal enough riches?

Any captain who was considered to be ineffective in raiding ships for treasure was removed from his post by his own crew, who could lead a mutiny against him!

What was the signal that a mutiny was underway?

The sound of a cannon ball rumbling across a ship's deck signalled that the crew was about to attempt to take control from the captain.

This happened to William Kidd aboard the *Adventure Galley*, but he hit one of the mutineers with a bucket and killed him! He was later tried for murder.

Doctors on board!

Pirate ships rarely had doctors on board. Sometimes, pirates injured a limb so badly that it needed to be cut off. In such cases, the ship's cook was called upon on to do the deed!

The captain's cabin also contained a bed and a footlocker for storing clothes.

Land Ahoy!

After spending many weeks and months crammed together on a stinking ship, with limited supplies of food and very little to do (between the brief moments of great excitement and danger!), most pirates were overjoyed to reach dry land.

By the time they arrived at port, many were rich enough to buy whatever they wanted, and soon squandered their ill-gotten gains on drinking, gambling and extranvagant spending sprees.

One eyewitness recalled:

"Such of these pirates are found who will spend two or three thousand pieces-of-eight in one night, not leaving them with a good shirt on their backs."

A pirate's work is never done...

In between the pirates' wild revels, there was still work to be done. Seaweed and barnacles clogged the bottom of ships during long voyages, slowing them down, and worms bore tiny holes that affected their seaworthiness over time. Pirates beached their ships while they were on land so that they could clean and repair the hull.

Why did pirates stop on land from time to time?

After travelling continuously for months, pirates not only needed time to rest, but also had to stock up on food and supplies. Most importantly, they had to bring their ships to shore for careening, or cleaning the weeds, worms and barnacles from the bottom. In their free time, they enjoyed spending the money they had stolen from merchant vessels!

A pirate lazes on the beach with a drink!

What did pirates eat on deserted islands?

When pirates pulled ashore on a deserted island, they looked out for animals like monkeys, birds and goats for meat. They chased these animals with clubs and sometimes even caught them with their bare hands!

Which active game did pirates sometimes play on land?

Pirates often had sword fights or duels on land. It was a popular form of entertainment for them. Two people would have a sword-fighting competition, while the other crew members watched. Duels were also held to settle disputes.

Where on land did pirates celebrate their victories?

Pirates loved to visit taverns or pubs that stayed open till late at night. They would sit there for hours, drinking. They were so fond of alcohol that they sometimes spent much of what they had plundered on barrels of rum!

Pirates often fought duels to decide who would be captain or how booty would be divided amongst the crew.

A pirate cleans his rifle on the shore.

FACT BOX

■ Pirates on land used a method called caulking while repairing their ships.
In caulking, the gaps between the ship's planks were fixed to make the vessel watertight.

■ Captain Kidd's ship, *The Adventure Galley* had no kitchen quarters. The pirates did all their cooking in a cauldronn, which was too dangerous to use in windy weather!

Why did some people welcome pirates on their shores?

e people did not mind pirates
ng them because they often sold their stolen goods at
per prices, and spent vast sums of money in the local
s and taverns!

Is it true that pirates often preferred to land on deserted islands?

Most pirates liked to pull ashore on isolated
ds, because they were not always welcome
aces where there were a lot of people.
erted beaches suited them, because
hey served as a good hideouts.

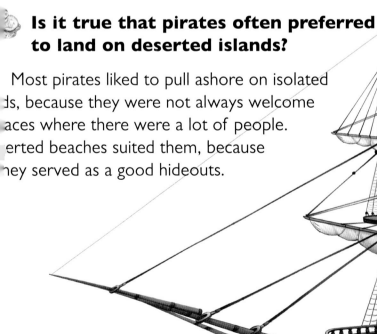

The Adventure Galley, also known as 'Adventure' was an English sailing ship, captained by William Kidd, the notorious privateer.

Land Ahoy!

A Spyglass is a small, handheld telescope.

Did pirates use spyglasses on land?

Pirates were always on the lookout, even when they were taking breaks on the shore. They would often climb trees and look through spyglasses to keep a look out for other pirate ships and merchant vessels in the area!

Where did pirates sleep on land?

Pirates usually set up tents to sleep in. Some pirates made their tents with old ship sails!

How did pirates make compasses at sea?

The magnetised needle of a compass always points north, so mariners can use it to gauge their direction. Pirates would make their own compasses by stroking a needle with a naturally magnetic rock called lodestone. Lodestones were often placed in decorative mountings to keep them safe and display their value!

Lodestones are naturally magnetised pieces of the mineral magnetite. Their importance in early navigation is indicated by their name: in Middle English, the word "lode" meant "journey" or "way".

What was salmagundi?

Salmagundi was a favourite meal of the pirates. It was a salad that consisted of chopped meat, eggs, anchovies and onions. Often served on lettuce leaves, salmagundi was also occasionally flavoured with vinegar and oil.

Always on the lookout!

Under Attack!

Some cunning pirates raised the British flag over their ships to trick their victims into thinking that a friend was approaching. As they drew closer to their target, they signalled their attack with a deafening explosion of cannon fire, before charging aboard the unsuspecting vessel, firing muskets, clashing swords, and chopping through the sail lifts!

After such a dramatic show of force, few sailors put up much of a fight. The only way to successfully counter a pirate attack was to avoid a pitched battle against these terrifying interlopers. Some brave crew members barricaded themselves into the strongest part of the ship and fought back with guns and homemade bombs!

More than 20 lead cannons could be mounted on a large pirate ship!

Which common pirate weapon was an early form of the rifle?

The musket, an early weapon commonly used by pirates, was a model for the present-day rifle. Pirates used muskets to fire from a distance, since they were less effective at close range.

The long musket rifle was usually fired from the shoulder at long distance targets.

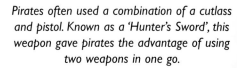

Pirates often used a combination of a cutlass and pistol. Known as a 'Hunter's Sword', this weapon gave pirates the advantage of using two weapons in one go.

 ## Which pirate weapon gave rise to the word, 'bombardment'?

Many pirate ships had bombards on board. The bombard was an early form of cannon, used for firing heavy cannonballs made of stone. Even today, we use the word 'bombardment' to describe a continuous attack with bombs, shells or other missiles.

The bombard was loaded with stone shots instead of lead or iron ones.

Why were pirate attacks successful most of the time?

Most pirate attacks were successful because their ships carried many more people than other ships of the same size. Pirates won battles thanks to the sheer number of their crew members and their ruthless methods of attack.

Did pirates carry a lot of weapons aboard their ships?

Pirates carried a variety of weapons on board their ships. Though they weren't always used, it was important to stock up on them in case of surprise attacks! Pirate crews never knew when they would be called upon to defend themselves.

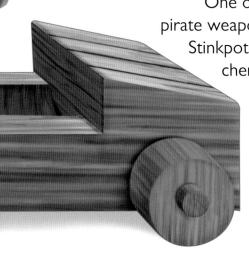

What were stinkpots?

One of the most interesting pirate weapons was the stinkpot. Stinkpots were pots filled with chemicals, which let out a bad smell when they were set on fire. Pirates would fling these pots on to the decks of enemy ships and suffocate their victims with the stench!

FACT BOX

■ Most sailors walked barefoot on the wet and slippery decks. Pirates took advantage of this and threw 'crowsfeet' onto enemy ships. Crowsfeet were sharp spikes that injured sailors who stepped on them!

■ Powderhorns were used for storing gunpowder. They were not usually taken into battle, as pirates loaded their weapons long before they attacked.

Powderhorns were vital because wet gunpowder is completely useless!

■ When pirates won a battle and took over an enemy ship they carried out a ritual called 'strike colours.' This was the practice of pulling down the ship's flag to symbolise its surrender.

What did pirates use to help them climb aboard other ships

Pirates boarding a large vessel would use axes to help them climb its hi
wooden sides. Once aboard they would use them to bring down t
sails - just one swipe could cut through rop
as thick as a man's ar

What were swivel guns?

Swivel guns were small weapons similar to cannon. They were so called because they were mounted on swivels (rotating axles) on the sides of a ship. Pirates could swing these guns and shoot at the deck of an enemy ship in one sweep!

What was the No Quarter?

Pirates flew a long red banner from their ship masts to let enemies know that they were going to attack. This signal was called the 'No Quarter.'

Was the blunderbuss a weapon?

The blunderbuss was a gun used by pirates for short-range firing. It had a funnel-shaped barrel that allowed the firing of several bullets at once, all of which took off in many different directions!

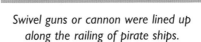
Swivel guns or cannon were lined up along the railing of pirate ships.

Which pirate weapon was named after a common house pet?

Pirates used a weapon called the 'cat o' nine tails'. It was made up of nine frayed lengths of rope, which were attached to a handle grip. It was used for beating prisoners and hostages!

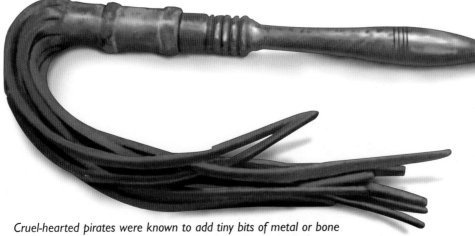

Cruel-hearted pirates were known to add tiny bits of metal or bone to the twisted cords of the cat o' nine tails!

Torture and Punishment

"*If one brother steals from another, his nose or ears are to be cut off*".

Pirates were a mean bunch indeed! They not only punished disobedient crew members, but also their prisoners and slaves. Sometimes, victims were tormented just for fun!

Cruel Customs

Whipping, beating and bruising – pirates were known for their cruel ways. Buccaneers were even said to hurt their prisoners with matchsticks and knives!

Dance of Death

When pirates were caught, they were usually hanged. Fearless pirates called it 'dancing the hempen jig'. They were referring to the hanging as a kind of death dance, on a rope made of hemp!

Sentenced pirates were taken to an execution dock where the gallows awaited them. This was a wooden frame with a noose tied to it. Before being hanged, pirates were allowed to address the members of the public who had come to watch executions. While some pirates appeared to be sorry, others shamelessly told jokes right to the end!

WANTED

Henry Morgan

How did law officials capture pirates?

Law officials had to look very hard for pirates and robbers, because many had hideouts that were very difficult to find. Posters with a pirate's portrait would be pasted all over villages and towns, offering a reward for information about the criminal's whereabouts.

What were pirate charters

Most pirates followed a certain set of rules relating to their conduct. These sets of rules were known as charters

Were pirates made to walk the plank

Pirates are famous for making their victims 'walk the plank' - a punishment that features in a number of famous pirate tales. In fact this was not a very common practice on board pirate ships, and would rarely have happened in real life

Walking the plank: this form of torture was used more by pirates in China than those of North America and the Caribbean.

What was the gibbet cage?

The gibbet cage was a wooden or iron frame in which the dead bodies of the most infamous pirates were locked. The body was first covered with tar and then suspended at a public place from the gibbet. It was hoped that this would serve as a warning to others and prevent them from persuing a life of crime!

Were pirates ever punished for their crimes?

Piracy was a major crime during the Golden Age of Piracy, and any pirate caught by a legal officer or the government of a nation could expect to be severely punished. The more dangerous a pirate was said to be, the worse was his treatment. At some maritime prisons in England, the bodies of convicted pirates were hung above water, and removed only after three tides had washed over them!

Gibbet cages were tailor-made, so that the skeleton would stay in place after the flesh had decayed!

What happened to rule breakers on board pirate ships?

All accused pirates underwent a proper trial to decide if they deserved punishment. The members of the pirate crew served as the panel of judges.

What is a "cackle-fruit"?

In the 17th and 18th Centuries, pirate ships carried hens on board to provide the crew with fresh eggs and meat. Eggs were called "cackle-fruit" because of the noise the hens made when laying!

FACT BOX

■ Most pirates did not treat their slaves and prisoners well and often tied them up in gang chains and ankle fetters. Gang chains were used to tie slaves together while they performed menial or physically demanding work, and ankle fetters stopped them from escaping.

■ Scotsman Alexander Selkirk was perhaps the only privateer to ask to be marooned! He later changed his mind, but by then his ship had sailed off, leaving him stranded! This story inspired Daniel Defoe's *Robinson Crusoe*.

Were pirates always sent to prison when they were arrested?

In the early days of crime, when prison cells were not so common, pirates were arrested and locked up in pillories or stocks. These were wooden frames with holes through which the prisoner would have to put his head and arms or, sometimes, his feet. He would be locked in the pillory in a public place, while people threw stones and mocked him!

 ## What punishments were given to pirates who broke rules?

The kind of punishment a pirate received depended on which and how many rules he broke. If a pirate stole from a fellow crew member, he was either killed or marooned after having his ears and nose slashed. Sometimes, troublemakers were tied to the ship's mast and whipped with the cat o' nine tails. For disobeying minor rules, pirates were either fined or not given their share of treasure.

To be locked in a pillory was a matter of public shame and was inteded to deter others from committing crimes.

 ## What was the worst punishment for a pirate who broke rules?

Marooning was a particularly severe punishment for pirates who broke the rules of the articles. It involved being left alone on a deserted island with very little to eat and drink and only one pistol for protection. Most marooned pirates died slowly of hunger and thirst.

Were pirates allowed to bring women to sea?

The pirate code of conduct did not allow any women on board a pirate ship! Only women who were pirates themselves were allowed to travel with a pirate crew, and even they were frequently disguised as men!

Pirates and robbers were sometimes locked in stocks instead of pillories.

Bring in the Booty!

Pirates might have loved their dangerous ways of life, full of battles, voyages, and adventures, but there was only one driving force behind every pirate - treasure!

Pirate Payday

Pirates of the Indian Ocean were amongst the most successful pirates in history. They targeted merchant ships called "East Indiamen" that were laden with cargoes of spice, tea, porcelain, silks, ivory, diamonds, and rubies!

When Thomas Tew raided a ship in the Indian Ocean in 1693, every member of his crew received a share worth £3,000 (at a time when an English naval seaman earned £1.00 a month!) Later, in 1721, John Taylor's raid on an East Indiaman rewarded his crew with £4,000 each and 42 small diamonds. One disgruntled pirate was given a large diamond instead of 42 little ones, and was so unhappy with his share that he took a hammer to the gem and smashed it into smaller pieces!

Some merchant ships were so full of riches that pirates could become rich overnight!

Bring in the Booty!

What kind of treasures did pirates usually find on merchant ships?

The 'treasures' that pirates plundered included grain, barrels of rum and wine, fine silks, sugar, spices, medicines, fish, wood, iron, slaves and weapons.

Why were pirates selective about the ships they attacked?

Pirates chose their target ships carefully. They selected only those ships that looked likely to have treasure on board.

Gold and precious stones were the most difficult treasures to divide fairly amongst the crew!

Did pirates ever find precious gems aboard ships?

Pirates were always in search of precious jewels and pots of gold and silver. They got lucky on some merchant ships that were carrying expensive jewellery, gold and silver coins, and gem-studded weapons and artefacts.

The fabled buried treasure of Captain William Kidd

By the end of the 17th Century, the diving bell had become popular for exploring shipwrecks and sunken treasures.

What is a diving bell?

The earliest diving bells, from 1789 onwards, were rigid bell-shaped containers which enabled people to be lowered into deep water while breathing the air contained within the bell chamber. They were used by archeologists and divers to examine shipwrecks on the ocean floor.

Was any treasure found aboard the only recovered pirate shipwreck?

In 1984, *Whydah*, the only known pirate shipwreck, was discovered in 1984. Amongst the treasures found on board were hoards of gold and silver.

Which treasures were used by pirates as money?

Pirates stole silver coins, called pieces of eight, and cut them up for small change. Doubloons, or Spanish gold coins, were even more valuable. A single doubloon was worth nearly double the monthly salary of an ordinary sailor!

FACT BOX

■ Pieces of eight were also called 'reales', and doubloons were known as 'escudos'. One side of the doubloon was inscribed with two columns symbolising the Pillars of Hercules. The pillars became a popular symbol of money and it is believed that the dollar sign originated from them!

■ Clothes were among the most common goods plundered by pirates from attacked ships. They would then wear many of these clothes, mixing and matching strange colours together!

Gold and silver coins were known as specie in the pirate world.

Bring in the Booty!

How was pirate treasure distributed among the members of the crew?

Most crew members received an equal share of the booty. The captain and the ship's pilot, however, got more than the others. Another share was kept aside to cover the costs of maintaining the ship.

What if there was no treasures?

If there was no booty then nobody in the pirate crew got paid!

Polly want a cracker?

It is believed that, in desperate situations, some pirate crews would eat their leather satchels! We know this from a recipe written by one of Sir Henry Morgan's crew members:

"…slice the leather into pieces then soak, beat and rub between stones to tenderize. Scrape off the hair, then roast or grill. Cut into smaller pieces and serve with lots of water…"!

How did pirates work on board?

Work aboard pirate ships was equally divided among crew members. This way, daily jobs were completed fairly and easily.

The pirates' charter of articles provided specific rules for the division of booty.

Did You Know?

From the barbarous Edward Low, who was said to have cut off a man's ears and made him eat them with salt and pepper, to the brutal Blackbeard, who stuck smouldering fuses under his hat so that he appeared in battle in a thick cloud of smoke, the pirates of old have, over the years, acquired fascinating, if gruesome reputations.

The Legendary Pirate

Works classic fiction like *Treasure Island* and *Peter Pan* created a popular image of the pirate, complete with pet parrots, wooden legs, hook hands and eye patches. Many writers turned these terrifying, murderous thieves into charming rascals or dashing heroes. Peter Pan's enemy, Captain Hook is even said to have been *"Blackbeard's bosun"*!

On the screen, as in books, pirates remain just as popular today as in years gone by, providing writers and dramatists with a range of dramatic possibilities. These raiders of the seas are readily recognised, and even admired as daring adventurers, romantic heroes, bumbling outlaws and, of course, as the black-hearted villains that many of them truly were.

This medal was issued to honour the German pirate, Störtebeker. Executed in 1401, Störtebeker, was known as the Robin Hood of his region!

Which pirate left a crew he captured inside barrels of herring fish?

The famous German pirate, Klaus Störtebeker, once left his captives in herring barrels! Störtebeker was the leader of the Vital Brothers, a group of pirates who were active on the Baltic and North Seas.

How did the Jolly Roger get its name?

It is believed that the name Jolly Roger came from the French description for early privateer flags, *jolie rouge*, which means 'pretty red.' The Jolly Roger motif of a skull and crossbones was first seen around 1700, when a French pirate named Emanuel Wynne flew a black flag with the picture of a skull, crossed bones, and an hourglass on it.

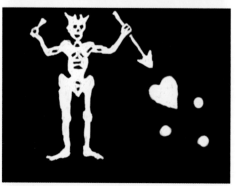

Did all pirate ships fly the Jolly Roger?

Not all pirate ships flew the Jolly Roger. Each pirate captain had his own special flag. For example, 'Calico' Jack had one with a skull and crossed swords, instead of crossed bones. Other pirate captains had a combination of skulls, skeletons, swords, and daggers on their flags.

Nearly every pirate had his or her own flag with different motifs to symbolise death. These included hour glasses, swords, skull, bones and bleeding hearts!

Did pirates smoke?

Pirates loved to smoke tobacco from long, clay pipes, but could only do so while on shore, because they were not allowed to smoke on board their ship. Pirate ships were made of wood and smoking on board could easily lead to a fire!

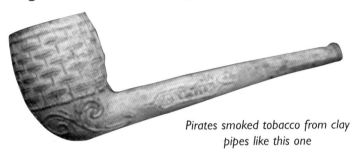

Pirates smoked tobacco from clay pipes like this one

When was the Yellow Jack flown?

The Yellow Jack was a yellow flag that was flown to show that somebody on board was ill with yellow fever or some other disease. Many sailors flew this flag to trick pirates into avoiding them!

What happened to pirates who lost a limb?

Pirates were paid compensation if they became badly wounded in battle. The right arm was worth the most, at 600 pieces of eight, an eye or finger was worth 100 pieces. If a pirate lost both legs or both arms, they were compensated with 800 pieces of eight and a slave to help care for them. Pirates were perhaps the first people to have introduced an insurance system!

FACT BOX

■ Chinese pirate flags often had images of bats on them. The Chinese believed that the bat was a symbol of good fortune.

■ Many pirate ships, especially those which sailed on the Spanish Main, were decorated with elaborate motifs and designs, carved intricately in gold.

Pirate ships were often beautifully decorated with animal figurines carved in gold.

Did pirates ever get sick?

Being a pirate was a dangerous business. Even if you avoided being killed, maimed, or captured in battle, you could still fall ill from diseases like typhoid, malaria, scurvy or dysentry. On a long voyage it was not uncommon for a captain to lose half of his crew to such diseases, which were rife at sea.

What did pirates believe they had to do to improve their eyesight?

Some pirates thought that piercing their ears and wearing silver or gold earrings would improve their vision!

What was it like for the children of pirates?

French corsair Jean Bart noticed his fourteen year old son flinching at the sound of gunfire during battle. He tied him to the mast of his ship, telling his crew:

"It is necessary that he should get accustomed to this sort of music!"

What was the highest deck on a pirate ship called?

The highest deck on a pirate ship was called the poop deck! It was usually situated above the pirate captain's cabin.

What were cannon shots?

Pirates had different types of shots to put through their cannons. The bar shot, which looked a little like a dumbbell, was used to destroy the sails of enemy ships. Even better than the bar shot was the chain shot. This was also used to destroy sails and other parts of the ship. With a chain attached to two cannon balls, the chain shot attacked with tremendous speed and force.

The bar shot, cannon ball and chain shots were handy weapons for pirates to frighten their targets with!